MW01243214

TABLE OF CONTENTS:

FROM THE FIRE

1. Here we are. Looking forward to the bright future shackled by our past.
2. The burden from our past is so fresh and unbearably heavy over our shoulders.
3. We are watching others enjoying life while we sitting here depressed and miserable.
4. Many people never appeased ancestors or entered the house of the Lord, yet they are blessed beyond measures and, here we are day and night deep within the Mpepho and incenses smoke trying every sweet word to appease ancestors and God. Even so the blessings are smaller than our prayers and offerings what is this life about?

We give big offerings and receive small while others offer small and receive big, it is like favouritism is at work here.

5. We are running around from pillar to post desperately seeking answers.
6. Through their readings, the Prophets and the Diviners are off the plot and don't make sense.
7. Clearly we are sentenced to Earth to figure things out and others are sent to Earth to enjoy life how fair is that?
8. Whatever reason that brought us here, is connected to who we once were in the past and what we have been up.
9. It is said that one need to remember their dark side in order to see the light.
10. I only see the vision of when I was a beautiful soul. Before I became dispiriting. Before I was given these body. The body with conditions, deals, pacts and contracts attached to it.
11. I was so exceptional and raw without flaw. So bright, so

daring, so fierce, and excellent, the true child of God.

12. Powerful magician I was with many spiritual gifts. The gift of teaching, the gift of telepathy, the gift of clairvoyance, the gift of clairsentience, the gift of clairaudience, the gift of knowing and making things happen. How I pray that I recover all these gifts of mine!

13. May the Almighty listen to my voice and answer my prayer.

I t is said that Light is established from fire and therefore light without fire is out of question.

1. In this case it means, in order for us to see the light from the void that we find ourselves in, the deep sleep that we are in, the envy, the slander, the shame, the fear, the anxiety, the stupor, the impurity and the passions that secretly nurse, we need to ignite the Fire.

2. We need to have the strongest desire to become the dragon with blazing fire or the never ending Phoenix that stood the test of time.

3. Fire, the power of transformation, the beginning of the true initiation into absolution and a God Head is all that we need

4. When one says "I want to possess my possessions", by so meaning they want to destroy that which would hold them or limit them.

5. Fire destroys the confining walls, fire resurrect, fire is the food of life, I am strong or weak depending on my fire

6. With fire I can see the light, I can rise, I will rise and I am rising!

~QUING TORCH

"Sedi la Tatagwe"

ACKNOWLEDGEMENTS

<u>To my darling husband:</u>

My sugar cane baby. My one and only. The one and only of his Mother and Father! The First and the last.

Thank you for adopting me as your best next of kin. Thank you for being patient with me while I was swimming with the fire birds, the dragons and hell hounds of the furnace and protruding my pain over you.

MOKINI, My patient KING from The Sphere of the NORTH, LENT-SOE!

You say let it rain and it lashes down!

Yours and mine resisted the tricks of men and the gods Mokgotsi!

<u>To my father:</u>

You see... We have made it through rage, wrath, pain, frustration and confusion.

MY HARD-HEARTED KING, SEGANE, HLABIRWA, TAU, TAU YA-MARIRI!!!

Let the Grace of the almighty appreciate all your hard work for this blood. You are my HERO.

Every morning may you say...May all beings be happy...THA-BANG! And we shall forever rejoice.

<u>To my Mother:</u>

Let your Heart relent. These deal was between the three of us!

May you Arise and shine and ascend your throne with Pride and joy. Let all beings call you Mmago-Tjatie for you gave birth to the

Sun. You sacrificed so much to beget this hot headed furnace of a child.

MY QUEEN! Thank you for marrying into this family. Thank you for carrying me to term. Thank you for taking care of me. Thank you for the role you played in ensuring that the blood of the Lions is purified and is back to its original form. You deserve your Crown and a peaceful rest now.

To the Earth keepers:

Thank you for your warm hospitality. Thank you for affording us the opportunity to work on our bloodline in your kingdom. I look forward to a peaceful stay in this kingdom while I continue to work on my soul assignments assigned to me by the DIVINE.

To the Lineage Holders

You fought tooth and nail and you are the most selfless, wise, tactful and diplomatic Beings I have ever worked with. In business Beings of your character are referred to as RUTHLESS business men. Exceptionally smart!

Thank you for the perfect map you have illustrated for me.

We are still to work together but allow me to say: Thank for your support, thank you for your protection, thank you for your teachings and thank you for the love and care to the blood.

Our work is still in progress...........

To the ALMIGHTY

The Most HIGH....THE FIRST and THE LAST

Thank you for the everlasting Seed that you are, THE CROWN!

Thank you for allowing me to expand from your DIVINE BEING in becoming this beautiful little tree that is continuously growing. My wish is to bear sweet mouth-watering fruits not once but for ever and ever...

I do not know what to say...

L et me just say "BAYEDE NKOSI"!

THE SEED

From his loins I, the ancient soul had emerged

A boy disguised as a girl

Many perished so I can survive

The "introvert" stern faced back then

Who hardly ever smiled or giggled with anyone

Only smiling and giggling secretly with my imaginary friends

He would look at me for quite a while!

He would sigh… and to himself he would speak,

"So much power on a girl? What a waste!"

His mouth would be filled with acid

With his lips he would utter the words…

"You were supposed to be a boy you!"

I would take one look at him and quickly look down

"You are a crook" he would sigh out and off he would go!

"I have to be careful, this man is on to something"…I thought!

He had so many bright "dreams" about my future

His Dreams not mine.

"You shall be a school teacher"

"You shall find a handsome hard working husband"

"You shall begot beautiful grandchildren"

Yo! Too much dreams for this old wounded soul to handle

Wrong Dreams this man is channeling!

I had to come up with a grant plan,

The best to change them all.

The ball was in my court,

I would go nowhere as the soul if I agree

My destiny was two faced

Like the introvert –extrovert I chose to become

Like the boy in a girl that I was

It was up to me to choose the right one

It was easy to follow the bright dream route

But I was very tired of the never ending circle of misery

The thought of being booted out of heaven due to karma again.

My heart was sinking.

The ancestors were in pain too!

Our chance of freedom was in these lifetime

There was no other time.

For me to get out of my temporary comfort zone,

I had to come up with a counter plan

I knew it was a very temporary life this one

Because at the end of the day,

These road and its dreams was leading everyone into the sealed caves

I had to do the opposite of every dream he had for me

I had to provoke him to his last core

Atleast that was part of the plan from the onset

Tact, diplomacy and Wisdom

To pretend as if I was clueless

When everybody is in their relaxed state of mind and unsuspect-

Quing Torch Mofokeng

ing,

Change the game plan for my bloodline's absolution

THE SURVIVAL STRUGGLES

1. In this material world the survival of man is based on the first principle: MONEY

2. Money is the ruler supreme in the 3rd Dimension. The illusion is that, with money one can build a house and feel safe and secured.

3. With money one can fill their house with furniture, food and all precious things then they feel "content and stable".

4. People believe that when money is scares, it is difficult to find love as a man or even find happiness as a human being.

5. Stress come from this constant fear of losing one's source of income.

6. Like a Johannesburger making peace with meat, we need to stop obsessing over money and make peace with it. It is said that "Johannesburg the city of Gold and Lights, the place of the never ending meat, where only the teeth of men peg out. Better make peace with money like a Johannesburger is making peace with meat.

7. Better we investigate the real reason we are here besides money for we found money here and we shall leave it right here!

8. Women who are broke are dismissed by suitable suitors nowadays for men are no longer ready to start off a relationship by buying deodorants for anyone's daughter.

One need to come nicely wrapped like a sweet lollipop.

THE TURNING POINT 01

1. When things do not go as we anticipated, we are prone to lament and we hopelessly flare up.
2. We then go around searching for the culprit who is responsible for our misfortunes.
3. People expect the Diviners and seers to assure them that they are victims and if they don't say it, they dismiss them as weak seers.
4. People run around towns and villages looking to pay other people to shed light about who they are and why are they suffering.
5. Life's disappointments, recession, loss of income, poverty, relationship problems, grief, poor health and bad luck can leave people confused, sad, bitter and angry.
6. One can become consumed by sadness and anger so deep and end up being wrathful.
7. When people carry wrath they resent others and sometimes even life itself.
8. Sad, miserable people quickly dismiss others and push away the chance to love and be loved without a second thought.
9. Sadness and victim mentality can change good people into bitter beings.
10. Extremely sad people and "victims "are in the world of their own, the void, and the nothingness. In their world they have no feelings.

11. People in the void, have closed up all their senses away from the material world like mad. They can't take advice from anyone for they know everything.
12. They are busy channeling strange thoughts, the thoughts out of this world.
13. They spend most of their free time eating their heart out, producing acid and having no clue what day or time it is.
14. In anger and wrath they are busy weaving and weaving non-stop they just weave.
15. They are weaving the strong nest of a jail and re-inforcing it very well.
16. The nest is supposed to be for the culprit who is responsible for their downfall
17. At the end of the weaving, after tying the last knot and cutting it, they are awakened to the realisation that they themselves are deep within the nest!
18. When there is no way out, they would go around their nest looking for a little hole to peep at the outsiders behind their back.
19. Through the hole of their nest they would see life going on as usual with people minding their own business.
20. Through the hole of their self-weaved jail they would realise that they are a failure for they have weaved nothing but their prison.
21. Witchcraft begins with a failure, a looser, and a dispirited somebody who had booted themselves out of the collective into a useless isolation.
22. In their useless isolation they have done nothing productive than to create hell for themselves.
23. In the trauma of their hell they become more cold and resentful
24. They design tricks to manipulate their loved ones
25. Within their frustrations they start to abuse substances and sex

26. They lie, they cheat and they attract more bad luck
27. A witch is the most unfortunate human being on earth for "everybody hates them"
28. Everybody is jealous of them
29. People think they are smarter than a witch
30. Everybody envies a witch
31. People enjoy sitting around and doing nothing but gossip about a witch
32. Loved ones are ganging up against a witch
33. The wrath that a witch carries is deeper than the ocean itself
34. No one can ever satisfy a witch's heart
35. One can roll down at the witch's feet and even kiss them, all the witch would see is tricks to trap them.
36. A witch is always convinced that people do owe them something.
37. They strongly believe that people need to be punished and taught a lesson
38. A witch is always looking for an opportunity to cause havoc and chaos in people's life
39. A witch does not wish to see people happy. Their heart bleeds when people are genuinely happy and laughing. That is why they like to cause division and misunderstanding.
40. A witch can never congratulate others on their achievements without adding a "BUT" or "however". After the "But' or 'however' comes a negative remark to spoil the congratulations.
41. The heart of a witch has a notorious hole at the bottom, no matter how many times one tries to satisfy it, it remains empty and dry. How frustrating it is to live with a witch!
42. Mind you a witch is not only a spell caster. Most witches don't even know how to cast spells, they are good at carrying a wrath! That is the type of witchcraft they do, carrying wrath!

43. There are two types of witches according to my observation: lower grade and Higher grade

Are you under witcraft attack?

1. When one realises that they are under the attack of witchcraft, the best plan is to conduct a track work on the soul level not Ego.
2. Expecting the Diviner to confirm that we are victims is a waste.
3. Higher grade witches expect us to believe that we are victims and we need justice so that they can play their game with us nicely.
4. Once one is engaged in those games, they should know that they too are witches, the lower grade witches.
5. At the lower grade one would open a witchcraft portal by running up and down the shrines, temples and churches shouting "back to sender", slaughtering chickens and bathing in dirty itching concoctions. Going through reverse muthi enemas, mpinda sweat lodge, mpinda purges and protection razor incisions attempting to banish witchcraft effects and send it back to its owner.
6. When all efforts are fruitless, one would find themselves naked by the grave yard or cross roads shouting back to sender and bathing on top of the tombs of the unknown.
7. When all seem fruitless, one would stand up and learn how to cast spells and conjure concoctions of their own. They are a real witch now.
8. All this trouble because someone got so angry and became ruthless? And another was lured into their nest because they believed that they were the victim? See how witchcraft got started!
9. The act of sending witchcraft attack back to the sender is a game of fools. Higher grade witches

did go through many sacrifices and abominations which a mere lower grade can never withstand. It is not wise to involve one's self in this loveless games for the troubled hearts!

10. A novice can never attack a higher grade not even from using reverse spells. When a witch sends a fatal spell they use their tikoloshi or zombie to send it. If it bounce back it will harm their tikoloshi not them. Afterwards the ever angry wrathful witch will be fuming and ready to eliminate who ever had injured their lovely tikoloshi. Be warned!

People are under witchcraft attacks because:

1. There is a witchcraft force within their blood:
2. Either they are begotten by a wizard or a witch.
3. Or they had previously used bad muthi and their blood is attracting witches
4. Maybe they were fed food mixed with muthi to weaken their chakras
5. Maybe they had sex with someone who used muthi on their private parts to weaken their chakras for love or to harvest their power.
6. Witchcraft game is opened for those who are willing to participate. If you are tired of playing with witches maybe it is time to look at shadow work.

A witch can go up to any length to satisfy their empty and dry heart.

1. It is said that after performing their abominations they feel high in ecstasy for a while then when the high wears off, they are back

to their misery to start all over again. Now who in their rightful mind would want to be involved in those games? Only those who are willing to play the victim and a doormat or a broom for witches can.

A witch can go to any length to satisfy their bitter heart.

2. A witch can zombify anybody it can be the uncle, the aunt, the grandmother, the grandfather, the son, the daughter, the wife, the husband, the cousin, the neighbour, the fellow brethren, the stranger at the bus stop, as long as there is access they can capture their soul and zombify them!

3. People who have survived witchcraft attacks can tell us many different horror stories about their experiences.

4. People's womb power had been stolen and been replaced with that of the old woman who is not even alive any more. Then the diviners see Ndau spirit. God have mercy!

5. Wives have lost their marriage due to endless miscarriages, unexplained infertility and bareness all because someone does not want to see couples happily married.

6. Someone as we speak is grieving yet another dissolved pregnancy because someone chose to remain angry and ended up buying a tikoloshi to torment happy people.

7. Someone was misled by their mother, that their neighbour owed them and was refusing to pay them back. In that moment

of gullibility they joined forces with their mother to bewitch their neighbour. When it happened that the neighbour was innocent, karma consumed the both of them. Their mother died. Now they are left in deep witchcraft practice shit.

8. Someone out there is suffering attacks because their grandmother left tikoloshis unleashed unannounced when they died. The poor soul have got no clue that they are suffering the inside job. And the Diviners are clueless.

9. Witchcraft is the loveless game of the troubled hearts. It all started with money.

10. During frustrations people fail to control their emotions

11. During rage people give away their power

12. In suffering people stop believing in Grace and integrity

13. When people cannot control themselves they want to control others

14. They become obsessed with the power that they do not have and they go around manipulating others just to feel "powerful".

15. They tend to shame others just to feel good about themselves

16. That is witchcraft on its highest level!

17. If one find themselves under the witch's wrath, better care not to get involved in their games. Better deal with the cause of the connection.

R age rises the highest vibration and there is no master of rage than an old time witch. One's rage can never match their witch's. Better throw in the towel and deal with what created the portal of witchcraft in one's life than to end up being zombified!

God did not gift us with fire within us to misuse it for witchcraft.

1. When people's fire is out of control they get sick
2. They are I and out of hospital and doctor's rooms carrying different medication without improvement on their health.
3. In order for us to work on our life's purpose we need to stay physically fit and healthy by mastering our fire.

Fire illness includes:

Low self esteem

Anger

Bitterness

Judgemental

Control freak

Digestive disorder

Bloating

Gas

Nausea

Acid

Emotional issues

Lack of purpose

Bad luck

Severe hiccups

Unhealthy Weight gain

Gall bladder issues

Adrenalin fatigue

Ulcers

Liver issues

C ontrolling the fire will lessen the above issues, if not one might turn into a witch.

The witches' nest is a chamber of never ending dark dreams. No one deserves to be in that chamber.

Witches lack the authentic connection with the Divine.

Higher Grade witches had created their own heaven

They have created their own "ancestors".

From their fellow relatives and loved ones they have created zombies

This "ancestors engineer false dreams to their target and they demand the never ending blood sacrifices to quench their thirst. Have you ever watched with awe people going through chicken, goat, sheep and cow sacrifices every empty moment? Yeah sometimes its fake ancestors sometimes it's because of the pacts...now you know!

Fake ancestors are those people who died practicing witchcraft. They have the realm of their own and still are up to their old games as ancestors. Those who are left behind to promote their craft venerate and appease them.

When one is possessed by those ancestors they become slaves to that kingdom. They carefully choose their victims under the false pretence of "spiritual calling". They choose those who are spiritually gifted. Their selfish plan is for their victim to forget about their soul mission and carry over the craft.

Theirs is the kingdom of hell!

Witches have on their pay roll: spies, fake lovers, fake friends and confidant whom they send to their target just to hurt them and gather information about their life so to impede their progress or secretly recruit them to their craft.

One should be mindful of strangers who burst out of no-where and become too open and friendly all of a sudden as if you have known each other for years. The arrival of this "friends" come with bad luck and, they are quick to find solution in times of bad luck. They would refer one to a "powerful Sangoma or prophet". All is part of the witchcraft game.

One should be mindful of the so called friend who does nothing but throw blows of negative comments and down-grading remarks at any given opportunity.

People treat others as doormats because they parade as doormats, therefore a doormat is a doormat just as a goat is for ancestral sacrifice. Who had ever seen a pig being slaugh-tered to appease ancestors in South Africa?

Goat is goat, doormat is doormat! Friends who play on their friends emotions are not friends. Allowing them to con-tinue being "friends" is like saying "hey, I am your doormat".

One should mindful of a new friend who is quick to share their life "stories", sometimes they are not really sharing but secretly fishing for valuable information about one's plans just to go report them to the witch.

After recently meeting a new "friend", what type of dreams do you see when you are sleeping?

Witches lack self-love and therefore they cannot love any-one unless they are gaining something out of them.

They are harbouring grudges and they are out to "teach people a lesson".

Most of them appear innocent. Interviewing most people who have encountered witchcraft effects mostly said it was someone whom they never thought or could never ever have suspect in a million years.

1. Anger make peoples lose their voices
2. In pain some people do suffer silently and remain silent forever
3. They develop shyness and they seldom laugh
4. A silent and shy witch is the most dangerous witch ever
5. I personally do not trust people who are quick to forgive.
6. They would never talk back at anyone
7. They do not complain
8. They forgive quickly and easily without showing any signs of emotions
9. They send mixed signals and emotions
10. They are secretive

I t all points down to KARMA!

Bad Karma started that moment in the past where someone lacked self-discipline.

The truth is always staring us in the face but the matrix of this material world is playing tricks on us.

We are so caught up in the games of this world so much that we are no longer able to access the Mind of God.

We do not hear our inner voice, we are judgemental and dismissive.

We are constantly in fear of losing our source of income so much that we end up being paranoid and confused

To make matters worse, people who are lucky in making strong income tend to belittle the less fortunate.

They look at the less fortunate as someone who has brought suffering upon themselves. Maybe they are right who knows?

KARMA

1. People do not know or recognise their God given abilities and therefore settle for less.
2. They carry responsibilities that are not suitable for them and end up being bored by them. They then sit around and become wishful thinkers for they know that there is more to their life than what they have.
3. There is always the element of doubt from the ego level in their thinking. Who can blame them because they are not good at track work?
4. Once they doubt their abilities they fail to come up with the better plan for their survival. They throw in the towel and lazy around.
5. In their laziness they start comparing themselves to their loved ones.
6. Instead of learning from them they become Jealous and bitter. Well some might try to learn from others but then who can offer that chance for others to learn from them nowadays in this "busy" environment? Only a few.
7. Instead of finding means to learn from those few on how things are done, they plot ways to destroy their goals.
8. They say "ever since you have found a job or a tender, you are full of yourself"
9. Where karma is involved, people's goals are easily destroyed
10. People have created strong future goals, yet they are shackled by their past mistakes. What goes around comes around that is the law.
11. When doors are finally opening and the future is promising, a lousy mashamplan out of nowhere would come

and destroy everything. It all points down to KARMA!

12. KARMA started the day a blood relative murdered a fellow human being

13. How many people did your ancestors kill?

14. Whatever transpires between the two people is inspired by the law of good or bad karma.

15. Things are the way they are supposed to be, if one feels otherwise they need shadow work.

16. Karma started the day a blood relative swindled someone of their hard earned money.

17. Karma started the day a blood relative made a pact with leviathan spirits.

18. At the end of the day KARMA points down to the BLOOD!

When the ancestor are lost and tied up in KARMA we are all tied up.

1. When they suffer we suffer for we are in this shit together.

2. For a major release and freedom to happen, there should be two chosen people to work on KARMA.

3. Both are of one blood and vibration. Positive and negative force, the head and tails, the saviour and their opposition. The dark bearer and the light bearer both learning from each other.

4. These two should carry their duties of KARMA with a very deep passion.

5. Deep within their work, they really do not see or know the true meaning behind their life.

6. These is the fun about these games sometimes. The fun to whoever is controlling the two bandits.

7. At the end of these game there is no one winner.

8. The two should both win or fail. The dark bearer should torment the light bearer very well for them to seek more light.

9. The light bearer should never seek help from the dark forces unless they are in the mood of throwing in the towel and joining the darkness.

10. The plan is for the saviour or the light bearer to navigate their way out through the darkness of their opposition towards the light.

11. With them is the multitudes of lost souls and spirits of the bloodline ancestors who have committed the abominations and are consumed by karma.

12. The dark bearer on the other is trying every trick accessible to impede the saviour from seeing the light. They recruit and bribe certain trusted individuals to be on their side , they raise the dead and use their ghosts to fight the saviour, they kill, they steal, they destroy... that's how these game is, intense, shameless and messy. Witchcraft on its highest grade.

13. At the end of the game, the dark bearer should be FORGIVEN for tormenting the light bearer. If not when the dark bearer dies, their spirit will be trapped inside the energetic body of the light bearer forever for they are one.

14. If there is no forgiveness from the supposed light bearer, after they passed on they will have no choice but return to earth and go through initiations or healing work to rectify AND THE LIGHT BEARER SHOULD RETURN WITH THEM for completeness.

15. We can be angry at all living things but not at our spiritual opposition or teacher. These is the one person who is always there in the dark to see us through the troubles of the soul. When we have seen the light we need to

return and carry them with us. That is what we have signed for.

To be able to execute our life's purpose we need our own genuine beliefs, not what others had instil in us. Well if those beliefs are right for our journey then no problem let the journey begin.

1. When spiritual change is about to take place, one would start dreaming of snakes. These signifies change in movement, a spiritual metamorphosis.

2. It is said that it is time to be your true self now.

3. You now have dreams whereby you are at school? You have a lesson to learn. You are to embark on a spiritual quest.

4. Look at how easy your life had changed from party time to anxiety and scary dreams over night!

5. I would say maybe starting from now you need to cherish and make the most of every blissful moment in your life because they can vanish like they were never there? Or maybe I am wrong.

6. Maybe stop lamenting and adapt to this new situation? After all you are not a victim of seasons.

7. When I am frustrated I take a deep breath and sigh out. When I was young I used to hate winter but now I sing my praises to all seasons.

8. To summer I say:

Oh summer most radiant season

I greet your sweet smelling flowers

As we rise and fall, dancing towards autumn

I can't help but love these sweat smelling armpits of mine

All because of you my hottest summer

I love you my beautiful summer.

9. To autumn I say:

Brown autumn, take my hand and dance with me

Oh beautiful colourful one

Allow me to take your hand as we walk together through change

To all the yellows, the reds, the oranges and browns

For all these changes happening will never change who we are

Deep down we are evergreen

Let us wear the red, yellow, the orange and browns and look extra beautiful

Afterwards let us wash off all the colours and see whether we will die without our makeup.

For the truth is, we should not wear makeup because we feel ugly

We should wear makeup because we are dramatic beauty Queens.

10. To winter I say:

The chilly dark nights of winter oh how I have missed you!

White winter morning with Smokey chimneys all over

The sign that everybody was ready for you

Who can steal your birth right oh beautiful one?

No matter how envious summer can be

No matter how jealous autumn can become

No matter how many tricks spring can play

They can never take away your birth right.

You are my snow white and my dark winter night

Winter I welcome and love you.

11. To spring I say:

Here you are oh my lovely spring

I am ready for you

Armed with all allergens and anti-inflammatory stuff

I am ready to walk the fields and smell your flowers

To meditate and contemplate on your beauty

To do self-introspection and plan ahead

I welcome and love you my beautiful spring!

12. See...the relationships with family, colleagues, loved ones, teachers and associates can be rough or smooth. People can be hot, cold, mild or windy like the four seasons. All seasons are your extensions and your teachers.

13. In every situation the trick is to remain content, to be patient, calm and understanding. To have the knowing and understanding that all things pass through phases for as we go forward in this trail of life, we are faced with different and difficult situations.

14. What are you saying to your oppressor, the witch, your rude teacher, and your ignorant parent or heartless mentor now that you understand seasons? I want you to write a secret letter to them. Do associate them with one or more seasons. See them in a positive manner. Say words of praises towards them like you would to all seasons. Pray for them.

15. What about those you used to judge? Or those you are holding the wrath against now as we speak? When are you going to release them? Know that releasing people from the bad space you have personally placed them in your good heart is a good start to your spiritual and emotional freedom. You are not doing anyone favour here but you and your beautiful heart.

16. Do you want to join witchcraft, can you live up to the requirements and expectations of witchcraft like sacrificing your beloved child, eating filth, stealing your older child's destinies and birth rights and giving them to your favourite child can you do that? If not then FORGIVE.

17. Does an aborted child hold a wrath against their parent for denying them the chance to live?

18. Whatever action the lost soul of an aborted child does towards their parents or siblings is just a cry for attention or help. After all they too deserved to see their point of light as the soul and the parents should arrange for their proper sending off and naming ceremony!

19. Oppressors and haters are just crying for help and love, and because we do not know this secret it is difficult for us to understand them. Instead we run around shrines and churches shouting "back to sender" and being consumed by a victim mentality while slowly falling into the same vicious circle of witchcraft without knowing.

Prayer to the Fathers who still carry customs and traditional believes. Ego, reputation and identity protection.

01. Girls who fell pregnant before marriage and gave birth to illegitimate children in their father's houses are faced with a serious struggle because of their choices. Some are forced into marriages.

02. Some are forced to abort, others are forced to give up their children, while others are living with the pain of being single parents without the emotional support of their family.

03.   We are a vibration. The daughter, especially the first daughter is the pride of her father. When the father is proud and happy of his daughter, naturally his heart would automatically produce:

- Love
- Joy
- Blessings and
- Protection

That is how his heart vibrates towards his daughter. Without effort. Just naturally.

04.   When the daughter falls pregnant without a husband, the vibration shifts or drops. To love, to bless, to protect and to be happy around the daughter becomes an effort. It depends what kind of a father one has. If he is a broken spirit or carrying a heavy load from his past life and the present, he will not even try to make an effort.

The daughter will automatically reap:

- Despair
- Pain
- Bad luck
- Disappointment

05.   Because the father is showing her the other side of his heart now. The bright side of the heart is hidden from the daughter. Believe you me it so natural for the cultural fathers to go this extend when their ego is bruised.

06.   The daughter might carry bad luck throughout her life. Until she decides to forgive herself, and her boyfriend for her decisions. Until she make a secret prayer ritual of forgiveness between herself, her parents especially her father and the Divine.

07.   The Divine kingdom is formed by the Mother, Father

and child. Whether together or in different towns, the three should spiritually live together in peace and harmony.

08. It is the daughter's duty to invite Grace into her life for her parent's heart to relent. It is the father's duty to find it in his heart to understand that we all make mistakes.

09. Hanging to the thought that other men are laughing at him because his daughter had tarnished his reputation will bring nothing but more anger and bad luck to his family.

10. We are so obsessed with reputation and what other people say about us it is so funny. In that process we hurt the people we love dearly.

11. When the first daughter of the house is rejected by their father, nothing good can come out of their father's house. The female ancestors, the main aunts of that household would sit in isolation on their verandas in heaven and mourn the rejection. NOTHING POSITIVE will happen in that household!

12. I have seen a situation whereby in order to fix that mistake of a daughter, a birth right was stolen and given the second daughter so they appear the eldest in the eyes of the aunts in heaven, just to trick them ancestors to bring back the joy and blessings. That trick did not work. People got arrested and spend years in jail. Suffering and shame continued to fall on to that family.

Bringing life to this earth is a beautiful thing. It is more beautiful when the parents are in marriage.

1. Bringing the illegitimate child to this earth is still beautiful but in Africa for some it is the beginning of the struggle between the mother and child.

2. Financial support can be there but spiritually there is a problem. Due to the customs and rituals that come with it.

3. In case of an African boy child, birth rituals can be

difficult or not properly conducted. The boy might be a troubled soul growing up as a man.

4. As long as we are still wrestling with the idea of putting some of the rituals and some cultural practices to the end, it is better we encourage a girl child to wait until they are matured and independent enough before they have a baby.

5. A Girl child should make sure that they make a baby with someone who is not into birth rituals and cultural practices if she is not prepared to get married to them but only like them as the sperm donor. Otherwise let her wait until marriage.

6. Look at the burden or stigma the illegitimate child is carrying over their shoulder and heart!

7. The problem is one with some boy children born out of wedlock...botched birth rituals or lack of in a place where it is needed

8. As humans we have created our own laws and customs, omens and abominations. This practices are programed into our blood. As the soul when I come to the body, it carries me with its customs and practices imprinted in its blood and there is no separation between me as the soul and the blood.

9. If the ego believes that without the proper rituals we are in trouble, then we are in trouble. If the ego believes that rituals or no rituals we are fine and nothing will harm us, so shall it be. One just need to stand firm within their beliefs.

10. One cannot be two faced or lukewarm. Today you believe tomorrow you don't, the next day you are back to your old beliefs.

11. I have witnessed many African illegitimate boy children who came into their mother's husband's homes,

changed the surname from the mother's to that of their step father's and lived a successful, blessed and fruitful life away from birth ritual drama.

12. When I say ancestors can be dramatic someone would say Torch is full of it. Ancestors were humans. The ancestral realm has levels. It depends what level of ancestors are you in contact with.

13. Even if I am chosen to fix the bloodline, I would still be careful not to be obsessed with ancestors for the route can be too karmic.

14. Not all ancestors need our help. Remember the deal? It is me, my parents and my children. Going backwards it is my parents as children, their parents and their grand-parents. That is where we should concentrate and how we should work going backwards deeper and deeper until thousands and thousands of years back. Depending on the length, age and level of KARMA

15. Beliefs and programs can make or break us as humans. They can derail us as souls for our ultimate goal is to evolve and stop returning here and repeating one thing over and over again. This nightmare has to end. This ancestral work should be the last job for mankind.

16. When we return we should be working directly with the Divine for all souls deserving ascension should be in ascension.

17. Sometimes the bodies we found ourselves in come with a lot of obstacles and baggage for us as the soul but hey...we chose this.

Blessed are those souls who did much work on their Ego in the past and are now in the well-polished bodies and blood. I congratulate you beautiful souls if you are still around this dimension, your work is very important for us. You are a good example of paradise

WHERE IS JUSTICE FOR THE OPPRESSED?

Now the light bearer and the dark bearer are freed and their sins are forgiven...what about those who suffered the effects of the battle between the two?

People where manipulated, people's gullibility was used, people were zombified and others suffered the effect of spiritual war in so many different ways.

Some wives did not enjoy their husbands. Some were left to be widows at a tender age all because of the spiritual battle.

All I can say is: this is the jungle, the survival of the fittest. A pot does not say to the cook hey...I am tired of being a pot and I want to be a plate. What I am saying is life is based on three things: fate, destiny and karma.

If one is tired of being a pot they have to join the fire and become the phoenix first. Then they can die and rebirth to become something they desire.

What I mean is the young widow chose the family they married into way back before they become flesh and blood. They signed for this family. If they did not like the conditions they were not supposed to sign for it. Better still they could have left from the beginning. When it gets tough to handle we have a choice of packing our bags and hitting the road.

A woman of flesh with her opportunistic mind full of games, would marry into a certain family with power and gain in mind. Only to find that their mother in law had already put the stamp and mark. They have positioned themselves very well in their throne so strong that no young bride can dethrone them.

It all come to strategy and proper planning. Not meaning the young bride did not plan properly. She did but she is not the fittest.

She could play all her games the way she want but once the ever ready and wrathful mother in law strike, she does not care whether it might miss and kill her own son. That is how the young bride would end up a young widow.

She should just hang in there, she should just admit the defeat, she should just forgive, it is just a game and she should salute her mother in law for she laid her foundation so well and strong. She would stop at nothing to defend her throne. If tables were turned, the same lamenting daughter in law was aiming that high but then she failed. And now she is bitter and lamenting...KARMA!

As for the zombified, once the two parties see the glory, all zombies and familia are given the chance to see the light too. Lamenting over the time wasted, lamenting over justice and wanting to see justice is a waste of breath. Life is based on three things: karma, fate and destiny.

Let us look at it like this...zombies were a dispiriting humans and they had to be removed from the face of the earth, be zombified and wait for the saviour to come show them the light.

As for the temporary barren woman and the one who lost their unborn babies to witches. Take heart and understand that those were not so beautiful souls you were carrying. They attracted witchcraft for they had the force in their blood. The Almighty is preparing beautiful babies who will withstand all the tests and pass through to your loving arms.

As for the woman who's womb power was replaced with that of an old stubborn woman who is already dead. It is revealed and therefore it will be solved. Right after working on your karma and bloodline witchcraft, your womb is about to be massaged by the ancient healer ancestors who well understand the matters of stubborn wombs and re-birth. Your womb is about to be bathed in the still waters of the west for absolution. Angel Gabriel is ready to put fire in that cold old stubborn womb. You are about to receive a well oil brand new womb. You can choose invitro or natural conceiving all will go well. Only after you have done much work on your soul!

As for those who were recruited by the witch and promises were made but not fulfilled and now they are gone to the light and you are left alone scared and wondering what will happen next. Survival of the fittest means others would be used as step ladders. What is left for you is to Repent!

As for the one who was lured into witchcraft due to being unable to control their emotions, it is really up to you. If you like it then it is fine, if you don't like it then confront your shadows.

As for the one whose birth right was twisted or stolen, do not fret for after working on your bloodline it will be released like sputum coughed up from the lungs of the Divine ancestors. This is the burning issue in the chest of the Divine ancestors that is waiting to be spat out and you my dear are about to receive what is rightfully yours without lifting a finger.

FINANCIAL KARMA

Karma is karma, I am just saying financial karma because I am being dramatic.

1. True wealth is not something that we should pray for. Wealth is this continuous flow of energy from the Source which is ready and waiting for us to harvest. It is easily reached by those who are bad karma free.

2. Making pacts with spirits of wealth is a way of taking a short cut to wealth and a very irresponsible one. It is not part of our soul mission to do short cuts.

3. Wealth is always there, like the flowing river of energy. People do get to it but do not get to it in the right way. They create generational Karma. That is how some families end up being forced to make pacts because there is no other way to survive in their bloodline than follow the footsteps of their ancestors.

4. Some families are as poor as dust because these spirits are there invisible to them and blocking their true wealth.

5. Making pacts is like you are say "I want all my life savings withdrawn from the spiritual bank to the physical bank right now"! Then boom... the spirit steal your money for you from the heavens reserve bank!

6. When you return in the next life there is no money for you for you took everything and ate it.

7. When you are born in such a family and decide to go against it, you are up for a big challenge with those

spirits. They don't make one rest .They want their sacrifices. To come out of such a trap one need to work on the bloodline Karma and contracts.

When I was still spiritually young, I used to assist people who wanted to do wealth short cuts by reviving their ancestral spirits of wealth for them. I strictly helped those whose ancestors practiced the wealth rituals before. Because it was a simple task of channeling the ancestor and the ancestor would reveal everything to us on how to do their ritual, with what, when and where and the items we should bring.

The day I stopped everything and threw all the calabashes into the river is when I met a very huge entity, white as a paper dripping blood in every hole on its face, with an unpleasant vibration like the ones in the horror movies which was so disturbing to experience. A ruthless entity which stole the life out of any living thing it came across when it was hungry. That was the end of my wealth pacts work. I closed down everything related to wealth pacts and chased away everybody who contacted me for those rituals. That was the beginning of my journey for ancestral karma healing.

8. Whatever one has done to themselves and their monies in the past it doesn't matter because with Grace they can request financial sponsorship from the Source. He/She can sponsor them or pay them spiritual grant from the heavens that will manifest into the material world until they sort out their soul mistakes and be abled stand back on their feet to attract their authentic wealth.

9. We can never go hungry when we realise our mistakes and redeem ourselves in front of God and ask for forgiveness. He will make a way for us. The children of God will never go to bed hungry!

FINANCIAL BLOCKAGES

So...your finances are blocked all of a sudden?

1. Not paying one's dues is a financial sin

2. Because everything that happens on earth is happening in heaven, a bad credit score on earth reflects in heaven.

3. Instead of requesting money in heaven to reduce or pay up your debts, why are people asking money to buy designer clothes?

4. How can the Divine trust one with a million when creditors are crying day and night to Him about them refusing to pay them a few hundred? Don't people know that the employees of those organisations rely on them to pay back the loans so that they can get their salaries? If we dodge their phone calls and come up with excuses not to pay them they all suffer financial loss and here we are sitting and shouting :I receive"

Don't worry I am not trying to be smart, I received the above advice from the source the day I was asking for the Divine to give me lotto numbers. As I write I am left with two entities to pay back what is due to them. Afterwards I am sending the paid up letters to the credit bureau. With Grace my score is healthy....

THE TURNING POINT 02

1. These dramatic spiritual shift bring forth new healers. Everybody is a healer nowadays. Let us not confuse it. Not everyone is supposed to be initiated. Some people are here to heal the bloodline curse. They therefore need mentors and healed healers.
2. Ancestors were humans. As long as they did not evolve they teach us what they know.
3. Unfortunately ancestors do not just ascend on their own unless they did work on their Ego while they were still alive.

1. Ancestors require our assistance to evolve this is why we chose their blood.

2. Most ancestors are evolving right now and they require less and less blood. Blood thirsty ancestors are in distress.

3. Same applies to ancestors who would want their child to keep on coming to the river for spiritual baths, those ancestors are unbearably hot and requires water to cool their hell fire down.

4. The permanent solution is to work on ancestral karma and pain not continuous visits to the river. What if there is another lockdown, what will one do with those ancestors burning over their head and shoulders?

5. If one's ancestors kill people for them when people make them angry or sad they need deliverance.

6. If one's ancestors would suggest that they mix some potions and trap a lover to love them more, they need deliverance.

7. If one's ancestors would introduce reverse spells into their work they need deliverance.

8. If one's ancestors introduce the spirits of Izizwe, which is muthi that is conjured with animals and human bones and blood, they need deliverance.

9. If one's ancestors introduce them to practices which are against human principles, they need deliverance.

10. There are entities attached to everything ancestral. It can be the beads. Iphandza (ndau plant) ighona (the calabash), bones, the baskets, the cloths (hiya) and etc. there are entities there hence one need to purify their items from time to time.

11. I personally have seen a vision of how some of ibaso in the markets (muthi ball for attracting customers) is made. I saw two men at ease conjuring ibaso, and I saw a bottle of human blood and fats as part of ingredients. Imagine you are the one using that type of ibaso in your business and it really works for you? How spiritually dark would one's business be? When the spirits of those blood and fat owners turn against them, they would blame their poor neighbour of bewitching them.

12. To heal the ancestors we need to remember. There is so much information hidden in our sub-conciousness that needs to be traced. The more we release and track the more we pick up hidden information valuable for our release and karma work. Diviners do not see deep family secrets. Only we can divine ourself through shadow work.

13. When we get hurt we numb the pain by hiding or shifting it into the back of our mind, sometimes we end up

forgetting about it but it continues to silently hurt us. When we die and become ancestors we become restless due to every hidden thing coming out to the surface. We become wounded ancestors and refuse to let go of the earth and evolve into higher realms. We become a troublesome ancestor who need appeasing of water and goat blood just to experience life in a goat.

14. In our healing journey let us remember that we are not responsible for everything. We heal what is necessary or assigned to us. Afterwards we concentrate on our personal soul mission.

15. We cannot entertain every ancestral spirit we come into contact with. Our vibration has a certain frequency that would allow us to work on certain spirits. If the frequency rejects the spirit let us not force it. It all take us back to: I, my parents and my children. We heal what we discover hidden within our parents, then we heal us for our children to get freed from karma.

GOD MISCARRIED MANY TIMES

BUT DID NOT GIVE UP, SHE MASTERED HER ABILITIES TO CREATE

When God realised that he was present, he did not allow fear to impede him from expanding to become who he is now.

Same as you and me. First our parents mingled and we became present in our mother's womb. From there we did not allow fear and anxiety to discourage us so that we end up in miscarriage. We allowed ourselves to expand. Our parents mingled and we created ourselves through grace. We saw to it that we were capable of working towards our goal to complete all the stages of development.

In those rough situations within the womb we did not give up. Our parents did not know what type of a child we were going to be but we took that decision upon ourselves on how and who we wanted to become.

When it seem so difficult to achieve certain things in life, we turn to lose hope and sometimes even give up. To give up is just a temporary stage. A child can be miscarried two or seven times but at the end of the day they know that they have to gather the courage and expand their cells to take a complete form.

God did not just wakeup and excel in his first creation. He struggled. He miscarried many times and was creating beings which were uncontrollable.

Our parents do not always excel in raising us. We turn to be uncontrollable at times. The only time there will be peace and harmony is when our parents accept that we are our own creators and they should allow us to create our own kingdom, our own protection, health and food at some stage in life. Actually a child who is allowed to be independent from a tender age tend to grow up to be a responsible leader.

Constantly relying on the help of our parents is what cause us fear in the unknown or unfavourable situations. There should come a stage in life whereby parents trust grace and leave us to it. When things do not move for us we can always go back to them for advice.

A woman who sees her adult son as the same little baby will bring nothing but chaos in her life and that of her son.

She tend to interfere in his affairs and end up being miserable. This woman should be careful not to let her imbalanced chakras block her from enjoying her own expansion.

If she continues behaving like that she might lose the chance of being closer to her grandchildren and that loss is like spilled milk. How useless!

God started mastering His creation the day He realised that we are all part of creation. He stopped controlling us His dear children and trusted us with grace.

God does not spend all day watching over us like a hawk, He let Grace Take control.

God does not behave like a mother of a boy child who had become a nuisance to the boy and his lovers by interfering. He wait for our invitation.

The only time God listen is when we call upon him. The only time He watches is when we engage Him. Still He is leading by example that we can do it on our own. We just need the light and guidance.

God is the first vibration. He expanded and we took form from him. Just like our parents did for us. They expanded and we took form and expanded on our own without them putting effort. We can do it at a certain age.

When things go wrong in life or when things do not want to happen for us, it is a sign that we are failing in our creation. Something is not right. We need to seek intervention. Just like God. When things went into chaos he shouted let there be light and it was there. Light was His intervention.

We need light, or enlightenment. We need knowledge. We need understanding. We do not need to be afraid for fear bring less or no production at all.

We do not always need to rely on external factors for we hold the master key, we just need discipline and knowledge on what we are doing. Mentorship increase knowledge. The problem is one, the mentor does not know us and our deepest darkest secrets. They can only feed us what we put on the table therefore one needs self-introspection and shadow work.

WE NEED TO MASTER OUR SHADOWS

When things go wrong, when we suffer:

Nightmares, anxiety, spiritual attacks, bad luck, relationship problems, unemployment, loss of income, unexplained health issues, infertility, miscarriages, mental break down, loss, and etc., we tend to go into a victim mode and start lamenting "why me", "what have I done to God" and all those type of remarks.

Forgetting that success is not through luck but discipline. Forgetting that if we do not wish for someone to succeed we are blocking ourselves to succeed too why, because we are one.

We are all the same vibration from the Source. We are from our parents they are from us. We are from God he is from us. We are from our neighbour they are from us. When we expand over the horizon we hold everything within us. If we take a look at someone and decide that they do not deserve happiness we are restricting ourselves of happiness

WE NEED INTROSPECTION

1. Who are we angry at, who are we jealous of, who do we hate, who are we envious of? How many people did we betray? How many people did we bewitch? Whom did we swindle? Whose marriage did we break? Whom did we make lose their job?

2. How many abortions did we do or how many girlfriends did we persuade to abort our babies? Are we making an honest living? Am I sure I did not commit a hidden crime? Am I sure I did not give false testimony?

3. Is it my authentic luck that I carry? Did my Sangoma or parent make me steal my sibling's birth right? Am I for all those type of despicable sin?

4. People who steal other's birth rights are doomed and are carrying two birth rights that clashes. Their generation will forever be doomed and in constant chaos. There is no remedy for this except to march into the Akash and plead with the Almighty to help undo that theft.

5. People who do not wish for others to get married are miserable in their own marriages if they were lucky to have one. Otherwise most of them are certified lonely bachelors and miserable spinsters.

6. People who tried evil spells to block others from falling pregnant have got crazy embicile children. If not embicile their children are so unlucky it is not funny.

7. People who do not wish for others to get employment do not have a strong currency at all.
8. People who wish ill for others suffer ill luck themselves
9. Whatever one wish for someone good or evil they shall reap exactly the same vibration.
10. When things do not go as we wish it is safe to look at the cause not for someone to blame.
11. It is very wise to always forgive those who trespass against us without wanting to know why they did it just for our sanity and good karma. And just because we all make mistakes and in our suffering, we tend to be less kind to others.
12. If we constantly experience the same bad experience over and over again, it is speaking to us. It is saying, hey look at me in a different way I am trying to teach you something. If we pay attention we will get to the bottom of the problem. We just need to pay attention, focus!
13. Sometimes we cry that things are difficult whereas it is us who are in a hurry for the end results and in the hurry we overlook subtle messages.
14. We need a proper planning, time, focus, discipline, persistence, perseverance and effort. And above all we need to master our shadows. We do not need to go into anger mode and weave nests!
15. We can only be truly happy once we realise that all beings in the universe including our neighbour deserve happiness.
16. When it seems like witchcraft battle does not want to stop, it is time to do a thorough track work and get ourselves released from the previous witchcraft contracts we have subjected ourselves to.
17. I am sure by now you have realised how easy one can fall into witchcraft trap and witchcraft is not only about spell casting and flying on brooms. Witchcraft

is also about reverse spells and shouting "back to sender."

18. If it is not rats in the back yard, it is eating in dreams. If it is not tikoloshi attacks it is night mares and bad dreams, if it is not bad luck it is drowning in debts. One fix this one or three problems emerge. Life is just a struggle and it needs to end right now.

19. Track work on the relationship one had with witchcraft in the past is a good way to put an end to witchcraft attacks.

20. Once they find out their life map they will confront their demons. The lineage holders can issue that map though dream work or channelling.

21. The starting point is the demon or tikoloshi that comes in the dreams. Finding the right healer to help one navigate the way backwards using the tormenting tikoloshi as the captain is beneficial.

22. Working on the ego level will always direct one to the suspected neighbour and the game will never end.

23. However, working with the truth and the light on the soul level will lead one straight back to the origin of the sin and their involvement in witchcraft. That is how one is released from that karma.

24. Reading books and downloading self-healing videos over the internet is fine but most people do give up and fall deep into the deepest void when those methods do not work. The problem is one, there is no healer. This work needs some healer.

25. I am against the use of muthi in situations like this due to the fact that muthi act as a numbing agent.

26. True healing comes from track work, from mapping one's history and confronting the shadows. Just study the behaviour of your parents, your uncles, your aunts and your cousins. The truth lies in them.

BORN IN A BLANKET?

Seers and diviners see a blanket surrounding one's spiritual body but the mother says NO!

When seers insist that you were born in a caul and your parents say otherwise it can be very confusing.

Just like when you have the water calling and they see the spirit of a mermaid but as a woman sitting on a wheelchair without legs.

Reading energies can be tricky sometimes.

They see the caul or white blanket but there was no such at birth what does it mean?

It means you came to earth followed by an entity. Sometimes the seers see a twin but your mother say NO! There was no twin!

The entity come with us to help us cope with human life on earth. When we are young we laugh, play and giggle with these entity (ies).

Some of these entities are from our past, they can be a past lover. When people make blood pacts, the pacts are very binding. Hence people suffer spiritual "attacks". It is not attacks per say. It is just a deal that one made with their past lover. When that lover tries to reach out we do not let them because we forgot them. Then they become violent and block our blessings. Then someone would read the energy as that of a tikoloshi. Hence I say the only person who can give a clear reading about their life is self. No one knows our story. We need to recognise our shadows.

When the seers see the entity as a caul, they would do proper rituals but the luck would still not open, WHY? Because it is not the caul they are seeing but something else.

ASK FOR RAIN ONLY AFTER INTROSPECTION:

When we were just a seed, everything was taken care of. We had the best soil, nutrients and water. There was no need to ask for anything. We had grace and we trusted the process.

Then we sprouted, to show off our true colours, we saw our shadows and we panicked.

We then went to the Divine for help and the Divine said:

"No problem, coming to me for help is good when you have awaken to the realisation of your colours and shadows. The first thing you should ask for is Rain and Sunshine D". As in for cleansing, absolution and purification. For light and wisdom, for resurrection, for healing, for food, for fertility, for the teachings of the truth, for centrality and balance. There is everything inside the water and fire. I blew up my air there and there is life".

"Rain and sunlight, these two things are very valuable in the life of every being. Hence the people of Botswana now refers to money as Rain. They hold rain with Reverence and respect".

Rain comes from the North, the Sphere of the Earth. Only the matured can ask for rain not children in age and in brain.

In times of trouble, when you have seen your true colours and are regretful, seek the fire and water for absolution.

PULA!!

PLANT YOUR PALM

"You come very far as the soul. You have seen all places. You have witnessed sorrow, pain, shame, abominations, joy, laughter, love!

You fought with witches, you fought with the ancestors, and you fought with the gods and some strange beings. You raised your vibrations with the aim to reach the heights of heavens and Grace descended to meet you half way.

Take a short break to integrate, to reboot your brain and always remember to share your journey as you grow. Books shall be written and there will always be the track record of how magical the authentic healing work is book after book. Just continue to share!"

Plant your palm. People are right in their own space. If a spade is Ace in their house so it is. Coming from outside into someone's space we just have to keep quiet and observe without criticism...

We only are to plant our palm in our space. Ebenezer!

Straight forward teachings inspired by Tlatlamacholo, the GREEN, the first vibration, Ramasedi the uncorrupted Gold and all beings of light from the Temple of Light and wisdom I say Bayede!

Email: quingtorch@gmail.com

WhatsApp: +27720883995

Green, Gold and Light!!

QUING TORCH

"Sedi la Tatagwe"

Made in the USA
Middletown, DE
07 November 2020